Sven Völker is an author, artist and designer based in Berlin. His uniquely playful approach to colour, form and typography has translated from global identity designs to large scale art installations, to minimalist stage design and picture books. He teaches graphic design at University of Applied Sciences Potsdam and is the author of *Some Book* (Lars Müller, 2013), *Go Faster* (Gestalten, 2010) and *There's a Little Black Spot on the Sun Today* (NordSüd, 2015).

A Million Dots

Published by Cicada Books Limited

Concept, illustration and design by Sven Völker

British Library Cataloguing-in-Publication Data.

A CIP record for this book is available from the British Library.
ISBN: 978-1-908714-66-4

First published 2019

A Million Dots

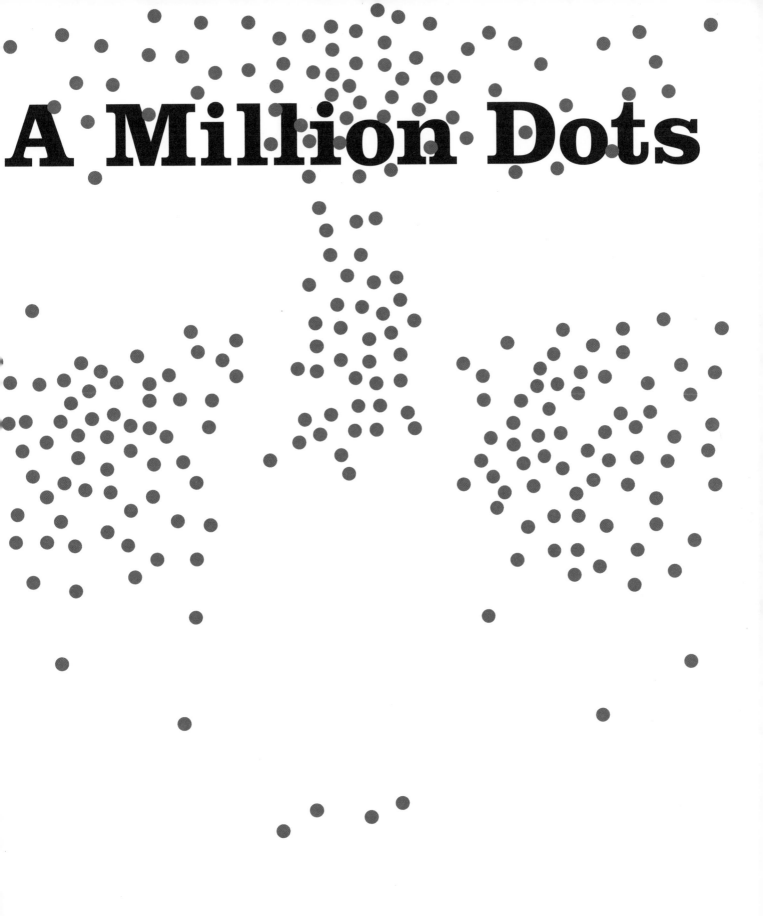

Sven Völker

one

1 + 1 =

two

2 + 2 =

2 + 2 =

four

4 + 4 =

eight

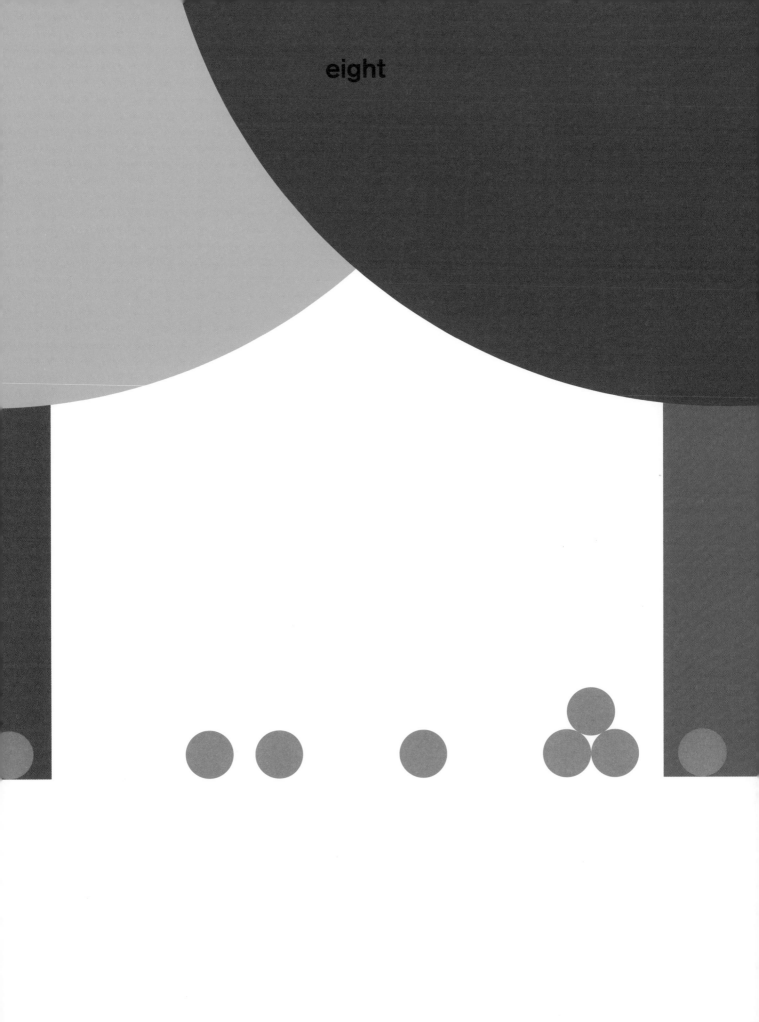

8 + 8 =

16

sixteen

16 + 16 =

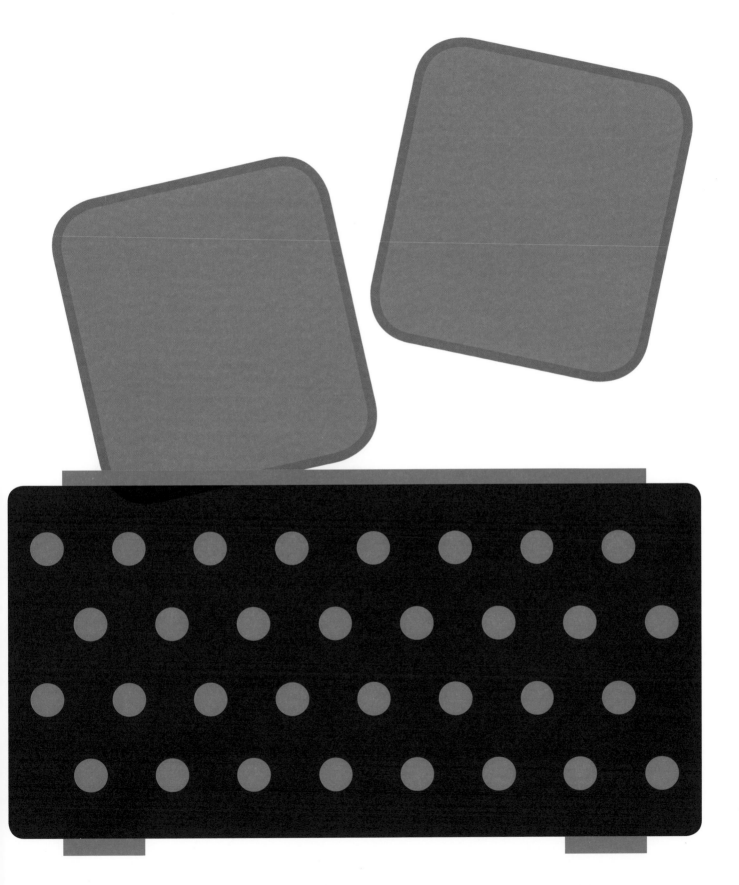

32 + 32 =

64

sixty-four

64 + 64 =

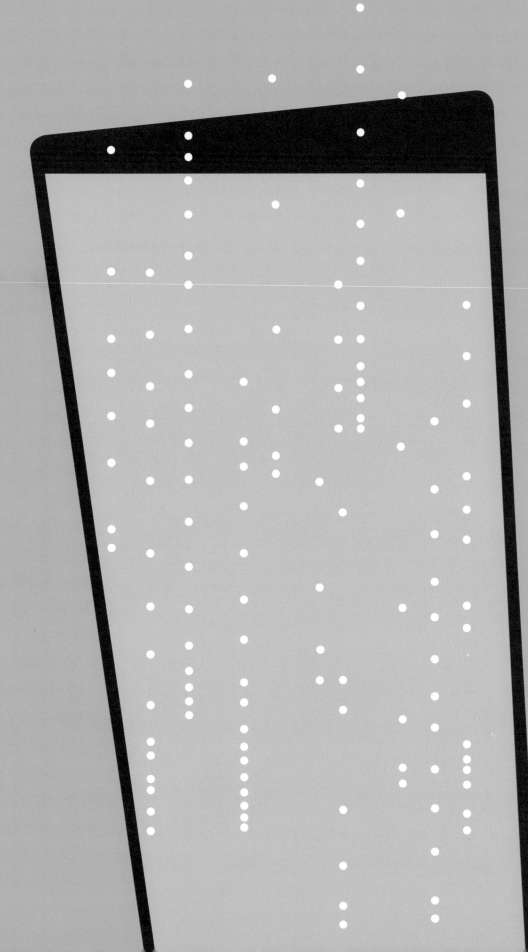

128 + 128 =

256

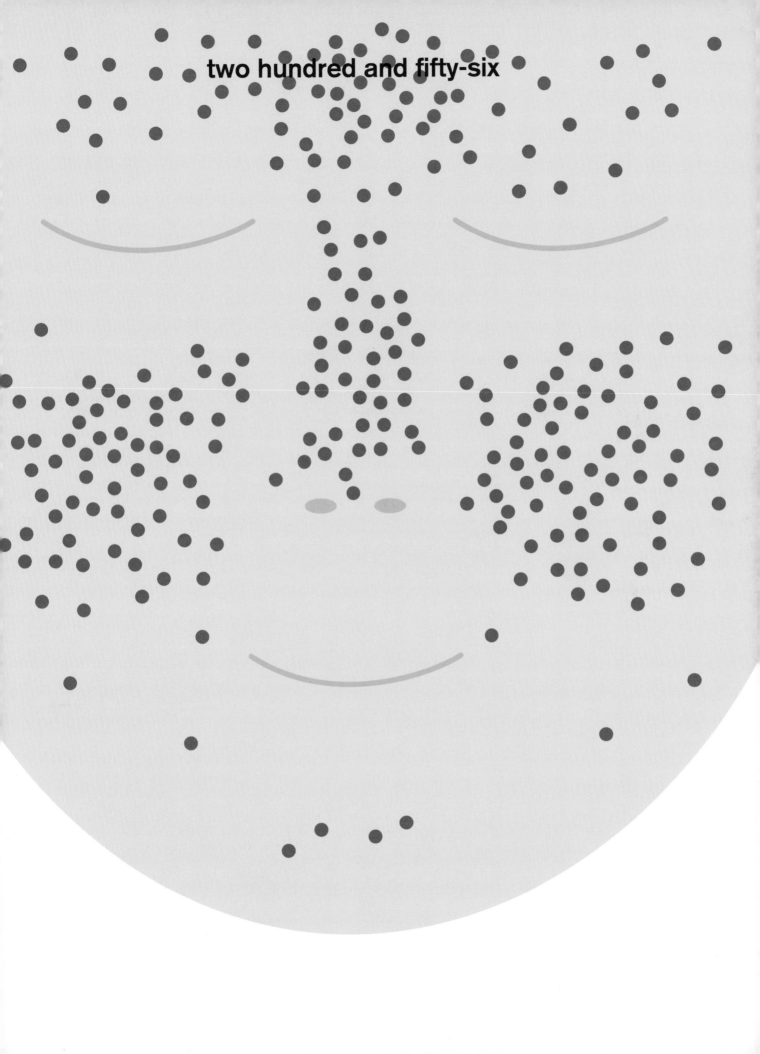

two hundred and fifty-six

256 + 256 =

512

five hundred and twelve

512 + 512 =

1,024

one thousand and twenty-four

1,024 + 1,024 =

2,048

1,024 + 1,024 =

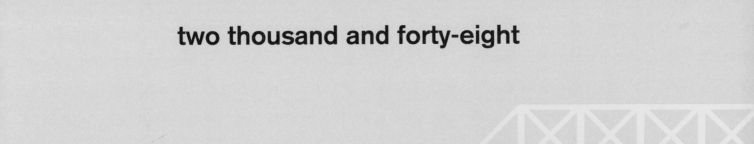

two thousand and forty-eight

2,048 + 2,048 =

four thousand and ninety-six

4,096 + 4,096 =

8,192

eight thousand, one hundred and ninety-two

8,192 + 8,192 =

16,384

sixteen thousand, three hundred and eighty-four

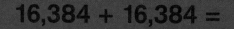

16,384 + 16,384 =

32,768

thirty-two thousand, seven hundred and sixty-eight

32,768 + 32,768 =

65,536

sixty-five thousand, five hundred and thirty-six

65,536 + 65,536 =

131,072

one hundred and thirty-one thousand and seventy-two

131,072 + 131,072 =

262,144

two hundred and sixty-two thousand, one hundred and forty-four

262,144 + 262,144 =

524,288

one million, forty-eight thousand, five hundred and seventy-six

five hundred and twenty-four thousand, two hundred and eighty-eight

524,288 + 524,288 =

1,048,576